INVENTIONS AND DISCOVERY

Henry Ford and the MODEL T

by Michael O'Hearn
illustrated by Phil Miller,
Keith Wilson, and Charles Barnett III

Consultant:
Frank Gasiorek, PhD
Henry Ford Estate–Fair Lane
University of Michigan
Dearborn, Michigan

Capstone
press

Mankato, Minnesota

Graphic Library is published by Capstone Press,
1710 Roe Crest Drive, North Mankato, Minnesota 56003.
www.capstonepub.com

Library of Congress Cataloging-in-Publication Data
O'Hearn, Michael, 1972–
    Henry Ford and the Model T / by Michael O'Hearn; illustrated by Phil Miller, Keith Wilson,
and Charles Barnett III.
    p. cm.—(Graphic library. Inventions and discovery)
    Summary: "In graphic novel format, tells the story of Henry Ford and his popular Model T
automobile"—Provided by publisher.
    Includes bibliographical references and index.
    ISBN-13: 978-0-7368-6480-0 (hardcover)
    ISBN-10: 0-7368-6480-6 (hardcover)
    ISBN-13: 978-0-7368-9642-9 (softcover pbk.)
    ISBN-10: 0-7368-9642-2 (softcover pbk.)
    1. Ford, Henry, 1863–1947—Juvenile literature. 2. Automobile engineers—United States—
Biography—Juvenile literature. 3. Businessmen—United States—Biography—Juvenile literature.
4. Ford Model T automobile—Juvenile literature. 5. Ford Motor Company—Juvenile literature. I.
Title. II. Series.
TL140.F6O38 2007
338.7'629222092—dc22   2006008187

Designer
Bob Lentz

Colorist
Melissa Kaercher

Editor
Christopher Harbo

TABLE OF CONTENTS

CHAPTER 1
THE EXPERIMENTAL ROOM

By 1907, Henry Ford had been making cars in Detroit, Michigan, for four years. His Ford Motor Company was successful and so was the automobile. People were driving cars in cities across America.

Every year carmakers build bigger and fancier cars.

Ford and his team developed a number of ideas for his new Model T car. They decided to build as many parts as possible from vanadium steel. This new type of steel was stronger and lighter than regular steel.

They also developed a one-piece cylinder block for the engine. Other engine blocks at the time were made of eight or more pieces and broke apart after hard use.

The gear system for the Model T allowed drivers to shift smoothly and quickly from forward to reverse. The car could be rocked back and forth to get out of ditches and potholes.

The steering wheel was moved from the center to the left. This change gave the driver a better view of oncoming traffic. It also allowed room for more people in the front seat.

SELLING THE MODEL T

In October 1908, Ford Motors introduced the Model T to America. At $850, it wasn't the cheapest car on the market, but it was the best car for the money.

15 MILLION MODEL Ts

In 1910, Ford opened the largest auto factory in the world at Highland Park in Detroit. It was 865 feet long and four stories tall.

FORD MOTOR COMPANY

Ford believed too much time in car building was spent moving parts, so the factory was designed to reduce movement. Raw materials were delivered to the top floor and processed into parts as they moved down to the first floor. There, they were finally assembled into cars.

The natural light helps our workers see what they are doing. With more light, we can put more machines closer together. And more machines equals more cars.

I don't suppose we'll have to turn down any orders this year, Henry.

With the new factory, Ford Motors made more Model Ts than ever. But people still bought them as fast as Ford could make them.

Why, George, you look polished up today. Going somewhere special?

No, sir, I've just been selling so many cars lately, I haven't had time to do much blacksmithing.

There goes another satisfied customer.

In 1910, Ford Motors built 18,000 Model Ts. But the factory still didn't meet the great demand for the cars.

By adding workers and workstations at the factory, Ford Motors built 34,000 cars the next year.

In 1912, demand for the Model T was still rising. Ford Motors more than doubled production to 78,000 cars. But doubling the output also meant doubling the employees. Eventually, even the huge Highland Park factory ran out of space.

All these men, and we still can't build enough cars for our buyers. We're four months behind in filling orders.

We'll have to hire more men.

We can't. We have nowhere to put them. We need a way to build more cars with the men we have.

The $5 workday was a huge success. Ford Motors was soon building 1,000 cars a day. In 1923 alone, the company built more than 2 million Model Ts. And by 1927, the last year of Model T production, Ford Motors had built more than 15 million of the world's most popular car.

CHAPTER 4

THE CAR THAT CHANGED AMERICA

Perhaps the greatest success of the $5 workday was that Ford helped create a middle class. Factory workers had more money. Some could even afford one of the Model Ts they built each day. They now drove the same streets as the wealthy.

BAKER

David, why don't we head out to the country? I packed dessert.

Sounds good, dear.

Soon, the Model T became more than just a family car. By adding custom bodies, people made them into taxis, buses, fire engines, police cars, and delivery trucks. Automobiles were no longer a novelty.

MORE ABOUT
HENRY FORD *AND THE*
MODEL T

 Henry Ford was born in Greenfield, Michigan, on July 30, 1863. Ford married Clara Bryant in 1888. Their only child, Edsel, was born in 1893. Ford died on April 7, 1947, in Dearborn, Michigan. He was 83 years old.

 On Christmas Eve 1893, Ford tested his first gasoline engine by clamping it to his kitchen sink. He connected a wire to the kitchen light socket to power the spark plug. Ford cranked the engine as his wife, Clara, dripped gasoline into the intake valve. As the engine rumbled to life, flames shot out the exhaust, filling the room with smoke and rattling the dishes and windows.

 Ford built his first car, called the quadricycle, in a brick shed behind his Detroit home. When it was finished, he realized it was too wide to fit through the door. To get the car out for a test drive, Ford broke down one of the brick walls with an axe.

 Early Model Ts were made in a variety of colors. But from 1914 to 1926, all Model Ts were painted black. The change was made because the black paint dried faster than the other paint colors. Fast-drying paint sped up the production of the car.

The Highland Park factory was nicknamed the Crystal Palace because the walls and ceilings held 50,000 square feet (4,645 square meters) of windows.

The Model T was so popular that by 1918, half of the cars in the United States were Model Ts.

The announcement of the $5 wage almost caused a riot at the Ford factory. Hundreds of workers from all over the country wanted to be hired. Ford made sure to hire black workers, disabled workers, and women, which was an unusual practice at the time.

The Model T, like a favorite horse, was often thought of as part of the family. People often gave their Model T a name. Two popular nicknames were "Tin Lizzie" and "Flivver."

GLOSSARY

assembly line (uh-SEM-blee LINE)—an arrangement of machines and workers in a factory, where work passes from one person or machine to the next until the job is complete

blacksmith (BLAK-smith)—a person who makes and fixes things made of iron

engineer (en-juh-NIHR)—a person who is trained to design and build machines

magneto (mag-NET-oh)—an electric generator that creates electricity to fire an engine's spark plugs

middle class (MID-uhl KLASS)—the group of people whose income level places them between the poor and the wealthy

riot (RYE-uht)—a group of people acting noisy, violent, and out of control

INTERNET SITES

FactHound offers a safe, fun way to find Internet sites related to this book. All of the sites on FactHound have been researched by our staff.

Here's how:
1. Visit *www.facthound.com*
2. Choose your grade level.
3. Type in this book ID **0736864806** for age-appropriate sites. You may also browse subjects by clicking on letters, or by clicking on pictures and words.
4. Click on the **Fetch It** button.

FactHound will fetch the best sites for you!